Published August 2021 Copyright
All material copy written and may not be used, copied or shared without permission from Kristie Lee.

All illustrations and photography images belong to Kristie Lee and may not be used by any means without permission from Kristie Lee.

Typeface: Short Stack Copyright (c) 2011 by Sorkin Type Co, Commercial Desktop Use - this free license allows you to create commercial products, Ebooks and PDFs - this free license allows you to embed the fonts in eBooks and portable documents.

This book is dedicated to my kids: Josh, Anna & Daniel! You are my inspiration and greatest joy, love you always and forever!

To all the single parents, you are amazing!

To my parents for always supporting and encouraging me through every season.
I wouldn't be here today without you!

My friends who never left my side, you are loved and appreciated more than you'll ever know!

This book is another victory not for just me and my kids, but for all survivors who dare to dream and live again!

When mom takes us places Daniel always seems to fall asleep.
He misses out on seeing all the cool things!
Anna and I are always trying to wake him up.

Hey Daniel,
"Did you see that?"

"My brother and sister think I miss out on all the cool stuff, but I think they are the ones that miss out!"

Just read and see all the adventures I have!

Hey Daniel, "Did you see that?"

I sure did....

I caught

a big 'ole

prize winning

fish from

the river today!

Hey Daniel, "Did you see that?"

You mean that

BIG

10 point

BUCK???

Oh...

I saw him alright!

Hey Daniel,

"Did you see that?"

I sure did...

TOUCHDOWN baby!!!

...and the crowd goes wild!

Thats a Big "W" for the team!

Those 2000lb squats in the weight room sure have given me an arm!

Hey Daniel,

"Did you see that?"

Look guys!
Super Daniel to the rescue!
Flying in the city sky!

Hey Daniel,
"Did you see that?"

"Oops...
well, he's asleep,
even in the
grocery cart,"
said Momma!

Oh YEAHHH....

I'm totally catching air!
Mountain soaring!
Country trail racing!
Snowmobiling life
is for me!

Hey Daniel,
"Did you see that?"

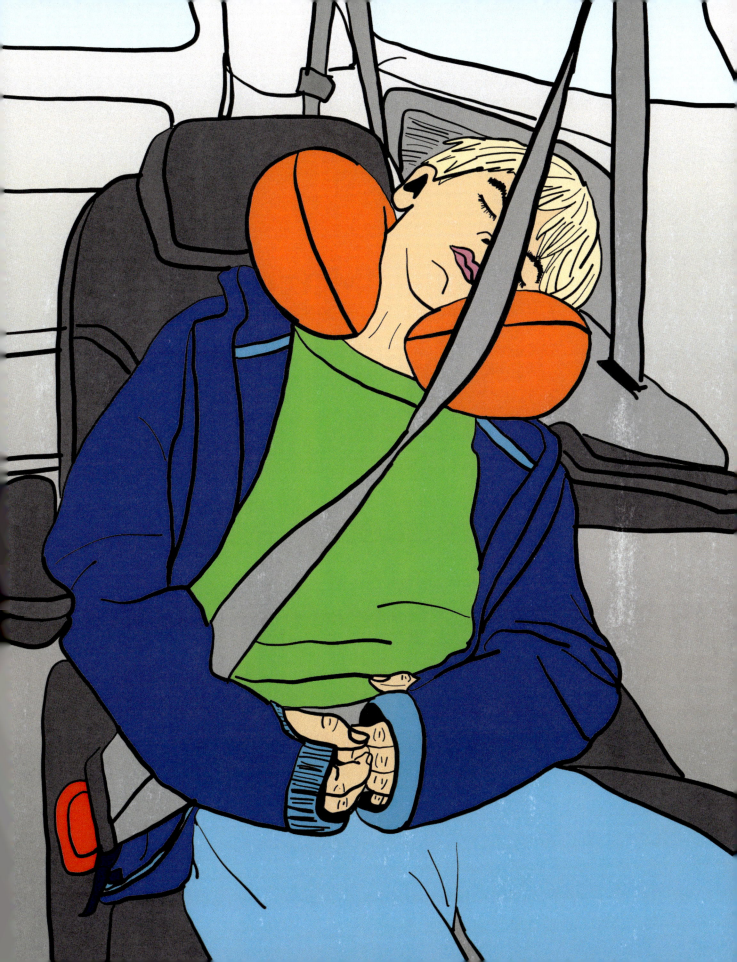

"Arrrgggg.....

"I did, Matey!"

"I am sailing the high seas with my treasure of gold," said Captain Daniel.

Arrrgggg!!!

Hey Daniel,
"Did you see that?"

WOWZA, sis....

I see a GIANT giraffe, eating from the tree! His neck is so long and his legs are super long too!

My African safari trip is sure looking up...
I mean, looking down!

Whoa... Hey Daniel, "Did you see that?"

Yeah, bro...

Watch me!

I am cliff diving...

free-falling!

Jumping right into

the deep blue,

freezing cold,

Lake Superior water!

Yeah... I'm smelling the dirt bike exhaust while jumping way up in the sky!

Wahoooo!!!
I'm higher than the arch... and number fifty-six is leading!!!

Hey Daniel,
"Did you see that?"

Yeah, sis,

I'm ridin' the BIG ONE...

"surfs up dude!"

Then I went scuba diving

and found an

old pirate's chest,

full of gold!

See, no one has more fun than me!

My brother and sister are the one's missing out on all the adventures!

"Hey Daniel, Did you see that?"

Now that Daniel

is a teenager,

he still drifts off into

his own little adventures...

even before his "big game!"

Hahaha... Momma life

is the best!

Kristie Lee

Adventure and creativity is an easy mix for this mom of three kiddos! The challenge of raising three (2 sons and 1 daughter) as a single mom was answered by her going back to her roots... enjoying her love for the outdoors! She is an avid hiker, runner, photographer, painter, and writer.

A Michigan born and raised girl, camping, stargazing, walking in creeks and climbing trees, she no doubt has a lifetime of stories to share. When you add in her kids and creative mind, it's a recipe with the best ingredients for adventure books. There will be more books to come for parents and kids alike to enjoy!

Choose the adventure & laugh often... dare to dream... anything is possible... have a little faith!

upnorthchic.com

Made in the USA
Monee, IL
05 November 2023